Petrified tears — who knows?

Also by Paul Evans

Current Affairs
True Grit
February
O.I.N.C.
Prokofiev's Concerto
The Manual for the Perfect Organisation of Tourneys
The Mountain Suite
Sweet Lucy
The Sofa Book

PAUL EVANS

The Door of Taldir

—Selected Poems—

Edited by Robert Sheppard

Shearsman Books
Exeter

Published in the United Kingdom in 2009 by
Shearsman Books Ltd
58 Velwell Road
Exeter EX4 4LD

ISBN 978-1-84861-025-5
First Edition

Copyright © Paul Evans, 1970, 1971, 1979, 1983, 1987.
This compilation, and uncollected poems
copyright © Nathalie Blondel, 2009.
Introduction copyright © Robert Sheppard, 2009.
Images on page 1 and page 123 copyright © Peter Bailey, 1977.

The right of Paul Evans to be identified as the author of this work has been asserted by his Estate in accordance with the Copyrights, Designs and Patents Act of 1988. All rights reserved.

Acknowledgements
The books excerpted here were originally published by Arc Publications, Fulcrum Press, Heinemann, Merseyside Poetry Minibook Series, Oasis Books, Pig Press, Skylark Press and Voiceprint Editions. Some of the uncollected poems in this volume were printed in *The Empty Hill. memories and praises of Paul Evans*, edited by Peter Bailey and Lee Harwood, Skylark Press, Hove, 1992.

The images by Peter Bailey are from *Schneider's Skink*, a limited-edition handmade book by Paul Evans and Peter Bailey, published by Near Zero Editions, 1977.
Reproduced here by permission of Peter Bailey.

The editor and publisher are grateful to Nathalie Blondel for her assistance with this project.

Contents

'Petrified tears — who knows?' by Peter Bailey   1

Biographical Note   9
Alive in the Twentieth Century: Robert Sheppard   10

from *Young Commonwealth Poets '65* (1965)
    The Valley   17

from *February* (1971)
    A Praise for Rhiannon   18
    from Taldir Poems   19
    The Hierarchies of Sound   23
    Launch the Mind into Space   25
    "You yourself are what befalls and astonishes you"   27
    Two Nature Poems   29
    1st Imaginary Love Poem   32

from *True Grit* (1970)
    Plans   33
    Instructions for Opening the Box   34
    Love   35
    Telescope   36
    Shooting Star   37

from *Prokofiev's Concerto* (1975)
    How Slowly The   38
    Variations (Mozart's String Quintet in G minor)   40
    Nachtmusik   44
    Cwm Cadian   45
    Polish Rider   46
    Broadway & West 70th   47

from *The Manual for the Perfect Organisation of Tourneys* (1979)
    1945   48
    Ode   49

For Barnett Newman	50
Two Sonnets	51
Dark &	52
The Manual for the Perfect Organisation of Tourneys	58
from 6 Watercolours by Peter Bailey	65
Of Gardens	66
Infamous Doctrine	69
Extempore	70

from *Sweet Lucy* (1983)
Sweet Lucy	72
from *Late Night Moves*:	
A Coupl'a Quips	73
Ode to Magnus Volk	75
Transport	77
One Way Mirror	78
Summer in the City	82

from *The Sofa Book* (1987)	88

from *The Empty Hill: memories and praises of Paul Evans* (1992)
Brightoniana	91

from *Romantic Relics* (uncollected, written ca. 1982–1986)
The Poet Virgil Suspended in a Basket	93
Lines Addressed to Ifor Davies	96
Half-Baked Juvenile	98
The Empty Hill	102
Talking with Dewi	111
The Mountain Suite	116
Two Pieces of Water for Sally	119
Romantic Relics	121

'The countryside, aflame with rumour'
by Peter Bailey	123

The Door of Taldir

Biographical Note

Paul Evans was born in Cardiff in 1945, where his father was a vicar, although the family moved later to Surrey. After schooling at Llandovery College in South Wales, he went to Sussex University to study English between 1963–5. With Paul Matthews he edited the magazine *Eleventh Finger*, which published many of the leading British and American poets of the day. In 1965 Evans married Rhiannon Davies, and they moved to London, where their daughter Catrin was born in 1966. From 1967 Evans worked on his M.Phil on Robert Duncan, under the tutelage of Eric Mottram. Living in Brighton again, he worked at a number of part-time jobs. In 1970–1 he lectured for a year at Essex University, where he co-edited Voiceprint Editions. His second daughter, Lucy, was born in 1971. The same year, *February*, the first of his four full-length collections, containing work stretching back to the mid-1960s, was published by Fulcrum and it received the Alice Hunt Bartlett Prize from the Poetry Society the following year. During the 1970s and 1980s—during which he published more books, including *The Manual for the Perfect Organisation of Tourneys* and *Sweet Lucy*—he worked at many part-time academic, teaching and bibliographical jobs, but chiefly administered the American Studies Resource Centre at the Polytechnic of Central London, where he organised important poetry conferences until 1988. In 1979, Evans moved to Liverpool, where he lived with Sally Evans until 1987, and worked both there and in London, including part-time work for the University of Liverpool and the Windows Project. Windows published *The Mountain Suite*, with illustrations by frequent collaborator Peter Bailey, in Liverpool in 1982, which dealt with his love of mountain climbing (his other love was playing tennis). His last volume, *The Sofa Book*, with illustrations by another collaborator, Peter Wilson, appeared in 1987. Evans married Nathalie Blondel in 1989, and their daughter Cecily was born the same year. Paul Evans died in 1991 in a climbing accident on Snowdon. His manuscript *Romantic Relics* remained unpublished.

ALIVE IN THE TWENTIETH CENTURY

Answering a question I posed to him in 1982 about his earliest poetic influences, Paul Evans replied, in strictest telegraphese: 'My exposure to unfamiliar poetry (which incs. Pound, for instance—already a half-century *old*, of course, by the time I came to it) went along with excited discovery in other fields—esp. music, painting (and sex).'[1] Confining ourselves to his purely literary discoveries—traces of the other fields may be found scattered throughout his work, whether Eric Dolphy, Casper David Friedrich, (or his lovers)—he was lucky to land in the right place at the right time, that is Brighton and the nearby University of Sussex at Falmer. 'I knew of the work of the Beat writers—esp. Kerouac & Ginsberg—by early 60s. Was introduced by Amer. poet George Dowden in 63/4 to Amer. contemporary work (a) 'Deep Image' poets Rothenberg & Kelly (as they called themselves then) (b) roughly, poets in Don Allen's *New American Poetry 45–60* anthology'. This anthology (I found questioning other writers too) was a common early and seminal discovery of the poets later called by Eric Mottram the 'British Poetry Revival'. ('I've always been amused by the religio-medical implications of that term,' remarked Evans, with his characteristically sharp wit.) Evans had the advantage of an extra-curricular mentor in the guise of Dowden, who lived in Brighton, and of his own enterprise while still an undergraduate: 'Early contacts with Brit. poets associated with "revival" ... came via classic route of publishing magazine with Paul Matthews (*11th Finger*)' (1965–68). This journal published Jerome Rothenberg and others, and also introduced Evans to the work and person of Lee Harwood, who, along with Matthews, was to be his closest poetry contact for many years.

In the earliest American poetry he read, he 'was esp. interested in Creeley & Blackburn (i.e. in terms of technique I was and still am attracted to "tight" "lyric"/"song" forms—though admiring those few who can handle extended "open" forms with skill)'; the last must include Robert Duncan, on whom he conducted postgraduate research. But it is with the other American Black

Mountain Robert—Creeley—that he shares a lyrical tightness and concision, but without the breathy, nervous lineation. Evans favoured flow rather than abutment, restraint rather than tension, crispness rather than emotional excess, wit rather than earnestness.

I first met Evans in the 1970s and published his work on my cassette tape magazine *1983*.[2] Recorded in his flat in Hove during February 1976, the set includes a reading of the then incomplete sequence 'Dark &'. I have always been impressed and moved by this meditative, lyrical sequence, and also by what Mottram called Evans' 'dry but intimate voice' on the recordings we made.[3] When Evans self-deprecatingly remarked, 'My own lack of stamina leads me to favour "tight" forms, possibly placed within a loose, ongoing structure,' he underestimates the power of his sequences (such as 'Dark &' or 'A Sequence', omitted from this collection on grounds of its length and indivisibility, but included in *February* (1972)). This serial sensibility also points towards the more metrical and rhyming sequences of *The Mountain Suite* (1982) and *The Sofa Book* (1987), but one should not forget that *The Manual for the Perfect Organisation of Tourneys* (1979), in which 'Dark &' first appeared, was a stylistically various book: precisely a 'manual' of cut-ups, collages, odes, extemporised poems; there is even a single poem in strict metre, 'Traditional: The Hidden Peak', which looked at the time like an isolated experiment.

However, by 1982, when he was answering my questions on the 'British Poetry Revival' and his part in it, Evans responded equivocally: 'I suppose I would place my work in this context—but not as an "open form" poet: I've always admired as many "closed form" poets as "open"—and in some ways regard myself as a traditional English lyric poet, with traditional preoccupations.' The repetition of the word 'traditional' here—we will pass over the word 'English' from this poet of deep Welsh inheritance—signals that he was already preparing to make the big stylistic leap of his career, to write in traditional forms. He seemed as bemused by this as were many of his keenest readers at the time. He told Eric Mottram on the phone: 'I'm into rhyme and wonder why.'[4] At first an evenness of line underpinned his evolving lyricism, in

Sweet Lucy (1983) for example, but by the mid to late 1980s, when he was working on the poems of his unpublished collection, *Romantic Relics*—which he seems earlier to have considered calling *Half-Baked Juvenile*—the inherited rhetoric of earlier poetry abounds. It seems to bypass a modern prosodic master such as Auden and return to the poetic form and diction of the late eighteenth century, and he was able to engage with the full range of poetic artifice in formal elegies, but also to pull this artifice inside out for comic effect. In the late 1980s, an era that was consolidating an image of alternative British poetry—say, in the influential Paladin anthology *The New British Poetry* of 1988, in which Evans is represented by four examples of work from *The Manual...* and *Sweet Lucy*, though it also includes a selection of five poems from *The Sofa Book* with their subtle, hesitant, almost apologetic rhymes—such work would have looked particularly idiosyncratic. Neither was it likely to have appealed to the poetic mainstream, which was consumed by an interest in prosy metaphorisation and a belated loosening of metre at this time. Indeed, my own repeated praise for *The Manual...* derived from my feeling that its stylistic restlessness was a precursor to a coming decade of radical artifice.[5] But Evans took another route, and investigated the radicality of artifice in the original sense. Read alongside Veronica Forrest-Thomson's use of traditional poetic artifice or Douglas Oliver's contemporaneous use of the stanza of the *Pearl* poem, this late work does not look so lonely—but it is still as unique as it was untimely.

I have approached the body of work Paul Evans left us for this selection with a number of simple principles: I have attempted to combine the best poems I could find while leaving some space to demonstrate the full range of the work chronologically, from uncollected work at either end of his career, and to show the full range of his poetry stylistically, from the free to the formal, from the surreal to the most objectivist. I have excluded the prose of *O.I.N.C.: An adventure story written to accompany 13 drawings by Peter Bailey* (1975) on grounds of genre. From only one other publication, another indivisible sequence, the booklet *Current Affairs* (1970), have I found it impossible to select poetry, although the ecstatic invocation of poem 11, 'it's exciting to be alive/in the twentieth century   the sun/ beating on your head tells you so', deserves to be treated (and repeated) as a motto leading into his poetry and its poetics.[6]

Asked how one's beliefs enter poetry, Evans replied to my questionnaire interrogatively, 'As translucently as possible?' Well he might question this because his poetry reveals a number of recurring themes, particularly the relationship of the human to the cosmos, of how consciousness fits in with the reality it filters, and of the responsibility the individual owes to others and to the body politic (and to its horrors on the radio, TV or in newsprint, which spill over into a number of lyrics). In a letter to Eric Mottram from the early 1970s, he expresses his poetics' stance toward reality:

> When I'm at my best, I don't draw or tear a hole in the world—there is an exchange between me and things outside me so much so that I begin to have distinct feelings of merging with the forms of earth, like the manshaped boulders, the cunts and breasts of the hills in Mid-Wales, the silver birches I know in the Mawddach valley . . .[7]

He opposed this to 'the Neo-Platonic view of Kathleen Raine, who gives so much symbiotic meaning to everything that we are bound to come out as mind-stuck-in-matter . . .'[8] There is—throughout his work—a general refusal of the guru-like posturing of authority-figures: personally, intellectually and politically, particularly in 'Lines Addressed to Ifor Davies', yet when, for example, he figures himself weeping at an atrocity committed on a child, he is self-consciously aware of the uselessness and even self-pitying nature of the gesture, even as he feels compelled to record it in one of his poems for '6 Watercolours by Peter Bailey'. Like Hannah Arendt, he recognises that 'compassion is one of the passions and pity is a sentiment'.[9]

This, finally, suggests that the self that appears in the poetry—an appearance several of his best poems agonise over—is very close to the historical Paul Evans that even the spare objectivism of the early free verse or the ornate formal distance of the late poems cannot obscure, although, as in 'Romantic Relics', the last poem of my selection, he never misses an opportunity for self-deprecation. But as Ian Robinson, the publisher of *A Manual...* suggests, in a comprehensively perceptive description of Evans, this too is a facet of the gentle and sharp man who wrote these poems:

> Paul . . . talked very knowledgeably about poets and poetry and people. Unlike a lot of poets, he didn't seem very concerned to push himself forward, and this, maybe, has something to do with why his poetry is not better known. My main impression was of a man who knew who he was and where he was in the world, but not with any sense of rigidity or portentousness or superiority. He was as he was, simply himself, whether one liked it or not; certain of some of his opinions, uncertain of others, flexible but informed and, I think, totally open to experience—all this allied to a nice ironic sense of humour, and a slightly sceptical attitude to people and the world.[10]

Robert Sheppard

---

[1] This and the unattributed quotations that follow come from this source, a letter to myself, dated April 19 (1982), part of my doctoral work on contemporary British poetry.

[2] The master tapes are deposited with the National Sound Archive, as are possibly the masters of Evans' unreleased Stream Record of the 1960s.

[3] Mottram, Eric, 'Paul Evans: A Personal Memoir' in eds. Bailey, Peter, and Harwood, Lee, *The Empty Hill: Memoirs and Praises of Paul Evans.* Brighton: Skylark Press, 1992: 66.

[4] Ibid: 68.

[5] My review of *A Manual...* appears in Bailey and Harwood, op. cit, but earlier versions were published in *Iron* 34, 1982, and *Ninth Decade* 1, 1983.

⁶ Evans, Paul, *Current Affairs*. Gillingham: Arc, 1970: np.
⁷ Mottram, op.cit.: 66-7.
⁸ Ibid: 67. I cannot help feeling that the word 'symbiotic' might be a misreading of 'symbolic' in the transcription of Evans' letter.
⁹ Arendt, Hannah, *On Revolution*. New York: Viking, 1963: 84.
¹⁰ Robinson, Ian, 'Paul Evans: A Book, Two Meetings and a Dream', in Bailey and Harwood, op.cit.: 85.

The Valley

When she crosses her legs
two pale moons of flesh appear
above the green stockings.

When she rises from the chair
they dissolve into dark water.
I follow her through the door,

Up the valley of white stone,
the moonlight upon it,
the fish in the silver stream.

Now she ties my eyes with thread
to the tips of her very round breasts.
She surrounds herself with the beasts of lovers.

Black mares graze with unicorns
in the moonlight, among white stones.

I close with her
in the bed of the stream
which enters my head at the ears.

I am water.
I have lived here before
with small stones in my hair.

A Praise for Rhiannon

When my woman moves
                    she does not
break into a thousand pieces,
                    into air.

Her body is of earth,
                  upright
on beautiful animal legs

like a creature of forests will stand
among trees
              quite silent,
                        one of them.

from TALDIR POEMS

for Dewi-Prys Thomas

*. . . epiphanies of the spirit there
and a chronicle of that time also . . .*

3

Keeping still
means stopping in the courtyard
with my back to the wall   .

A tree screams
inwardly, as an owl shifts
in the branches   .

All night I heard him
breathing on my pillow   .

Now he listens to my heart
beating in the yard   .

4

A black cow, carrying
the hill on its horns, breaks
the green ferns down.

                                        Distant confusion
                                        of insects
                                        breeds in the ear.

All sounds concur.

The curved horn
tears the earth,
loose rock follows.

Scared birds
leave the area, rising
on her cry.

She is calling
for two companions
left behind,

black beast
weeping
on a green hillside.

6 *For Rhys*

Dead, left in
the dark after battle,
return to stone,

leaving no trace
of blood, breath
or bone.

Only the rain
seeps
through the heaped-up stones.

This night
a certain light
dropped down,

releasing that
withheld by them
so long, making

these warriors' bodies
gleam again
from stone.

7

A pair of boots,
a jacket.

Cracked
at the root they found him,

bright ice
curled round him,

frost
in his pocket.

No creature
crept near to disturb him,

scared by fire
when the moon was upon him.

9

*The lifting of clouds
is the work of gods,
the raising of clouds
produces gold.*

No longer white, the fields dazzle.
The lower slopes vibrate
as golden sheep
cross and recross them.

Blades of light start up
from openings in the field
where the full light moves
beyond the pine-enclosure.

This is the vision we have waited
Children watch
in pure amazement
from the windows of Ty'n Llidiart.

We see that gold
the Masters told us
was a symbol for the soul
and its light plays over us.

*The lifting of clouds
is the work of gods,
the raising of clouds
produces gold.*

The Hierarchies of Sound

Just the slightest
clink of a cinder
      in the fire
      dying down
woke my mind. I was reading
      a poem where
      the poet says
'it was the sound of a fire
on the hearth . . . sparks
      of delight.'

           It woke me
and flared to a memory,
where I was sitting
      by the Thames
      at Chiswick Eyot,
            listening

to the clink
      of a rusty tin
      scraping the shore,
pushed in
      by a ripple
      on a ripple. The scrape

of metal on stone
woke me to the
hierarchies of sound. Sparks
      of delight!

           A gull flew
into midstream from the shore,

wingtips hitting the water,
      a heavy sound.

I was listening
to the sound of the fire
      in a poem
when the clink of a cinder—
or was it a tin?—
plunged me in the silence
      of the river.

Launch the Mind into Space

or drop down
                    gulfs of the body,
you will find company.

But the bones of my left foot
are so far away from my mind,
they know nothing
                    of each other.

The messengers move
on unmapped roads
with the speed of blood.
I have no check
on their movements.
They get their orders
                    elsewhere,
electrical charges
and secret impulses—

the current streams.

Whitman was right:
The body is electric.
                    It crackles
with energy from space.
My heart, my lungs, my
intestinal tracts—strange
meteors lodged there, coils
of the serpent Ourobouros
whose tail is in his mouth,
whose body circles the universe.

Or maybe his body is
the universe
and we all—stars, plants,
creatures—merely fall
out through his arse
into his mouth again
till the whole vast
being decays, and then . . .

a memory this poem dragged out
is lost now in the brain-coil—
something I ate for lunch
is stuck, light years away,
in the great intestine—
the sun, too, is dying,
losing its light in
the serpent's belly

.

Do you believe in beings
      from outer space?
I do. And in beings who
      live inside me,
who leave their traces
in bone and flesh-strata.

They are the angels el-Arabi tells us
'are the powers hidden
in the organs and faculties of man.'
And Jalaludin Rumi says
they only respond
              to necessity.

'You yourself are what befalls and astonishes you' (Nietzsche)

for Eric Mottram

1

Bach on the record player
announces Order—
      in his mind only?
      or did he stumble
           by chance
      on the Order containing
           all orders?

(The music an offering
     of itself
up to the source of music:

perpetual canon re-
sounding in the spaces
where Chance rules the stars:

      galaxies passing through each other,
      a thousand million suns shifting
      positions without grazing their skins.)

Chance rules the stars?

      are asymmetric forms
      evidence of total asymmetry?
      is what-is-there
      limited to our discovery
      or can it contain
      disparate multitudes?

2

I was working in the garden
under the slope of the mountain
all day, cutting back
a year's grass. Bees dropped
the soft sound of their work
in the air. A cluster
attended the flowering privet,
shaking the whiteness there.
                         Was it
Chance turned my head, catching
a warmth the flowers offered,
as if they would make me a gift
of heat they had from the daylong sun?

3

I thought to draw a new music
from the poem, blind to its source
         in myself. Bound to it,
I missed the flowers you had placed
in the room, white exploding
         out of the blue

and falling, fell into myself,
         astonishing me

and the blue eyes of my daughter
watching me write, her small body
a whiteness moving   in
         and out of the sun.

Two Nature Poems

1 Rumbling Kern

for J. T. White

Places like Rumbling Kern make us happy
with wind and differential erosion. Often,
on stormy nights, we've sat there thinking
how rocks wear away at different rates
before the onslaught of waves and weather,
but none so fast as the human heart
when love's foaming fingers test its beaches.

South of Craster, the sea has produced
a ribbed effect, where thin shale bands
erode into hollows. We nearly got caught
by the incoming tide, but had enough time
to admire the pothole's natural sculpture.
Each held, trapped in their oscillation,
the stones which gouged these smooth sockets.

So we ourselves, on the islands
we inhabit, to white bones wither,
useless as stars on a clear night
to a traveller who's lost his star-map.

2 Four Ways of Looking at an English Landscape

for L. P. Samuels

1

While waiting for help to arrive
we had the leisure to admire
the golden foliage of the oaks,
half-concealing precipitous crags
on the sandstone escarpment.
Robins sang, and the first thrush.
A flock of redwings flew overhead
to land in a hedge stained with crimson.

2

Your breath is easily taken away
by the lovely Peckforton Hills
in the last week in November.
At all the rookeries we passed
till we broke the accelerator cable
the birds were about their nests,
'filling the air with the hoarse noise
that most of all is England's voice'.

3

The nests were many and various
as islands in an archipelago
where oak is the dominant tree.
The countryside was more robust
than we were led to expect, but
no-one knew the real purpose
of the rooks' autumnal assemblies
anymore than the rooks themselves.

4

We broke down on a drive
east to west across Cheshire.
Being for the most part city-folk,
the social habits of the birds
escaped us. What we really liked
was the way the wind blew in our faces,
setting our teeth on edge
and flouting convention.

1ST IMAGINARY LOVE POEM

Your hair a nest of colours a tree
the sky hung from you constantly
amaze me new dialects and everything
the white clouds drifting in your eyes

'I like poetry as much as sleeping' you said
and the guards lined up outside the tower
the crocodiles were all on form that day
wiping your face in the sun

how could I fail to love you for what you did?
bending to pick up the message
my hours of waiting destroyed 'Meet me
by the equestrian statue at 2 o'clock'

it was an English sunset the bells
in my sleep reminding me of home
I shall be there fully-dressed and awake
their jaws snapping and the water turning red

Plans

for Catrin

all the poems I wrote while asleep
have left my head   images
melted in the light of day

the toy plane with yellow wings
revs up and rolls out
onto the mat   but the pilot
has forgotten his instructions
and turns back   later

breakfast is eaten and plans are laid

later still   a picnic is eaten
by a lake

at last   the plane takes off
and is never seen again

Instructions for Opening the Box

shadows lengthen   the quiet square
the gates all closed   finally
there's nothing to explain

this box I give you   open it only
in direst need   light on your face
destroys it   this time of year   wind

ruffling the shadows on the sea
I make a building of my hate
to lose you in   open it only

in broad day   nothing is explained
finally   all those words of
poetry   stuck in my throat

Love

it opens and shuts like a door in the wind
keeping the nervous system alive up here
in the window in the cloud where I write

downstairs the kettles are boiling keeping time
but here the air is full of air
continuously involved in the loops of my pen

as I watch you moving through the day
on the screen of the sky outside my head
infinite by definition   o mortals!

TELESCOPE

put 6d. in the slot

the panorama
takes your breath away
surrounded by hills
ocean on the left

now you know why the girl you're with
wears her hair like she does
it suits her too

off/on   the beautiful unfolds
through all the possibilities of blue

you focus
on a small figure far below
window-shopping on Princes St.

and follow him
till the money runs out

Shooting Star

for Peter

Give this to the girl who has just caught the shooting star
in your picture on the wall of your room   I hope
she will wear it like a jewel in the quiet
which is not really quiet when you're asleep

and all the other heavenly bodies
one of whom sits in the next room all day
drawing the special star that is hers   yours too
mine's up here for a moment lost in the clouds

if only the astrologers were right   no
if only the astrologers were wrong
then I could avoid the terrible calamity
they keep on hinting about   money for sure

who cares   horoscope's only a long word
for fear   and we gave that up long ago

How Slowly The

1

How slowly the
world comes back

built up again
from limbs tangled on a bed

quiet sounds
of breathing.

Stroke me.
You won't hurt me.

This is a moment
I am not holding

unless by the power of
my gaze alone.

2

Behind your face
I catch what

faces,
watching me

with care,
as all of mine

watch you—
the care, I mean

that love has
for the world.

3

You are the force that draws
these words from me

as spring sends the green stuff
shooting up the new stems

in the old poetry, or girders sprout
all along the seafront blocks

to be modern. Because of you
I break the icy grip

of the urge to be perfect
that froze my words so long.

VARIATIONS (Mozart's String Quintet in G minor)

> In all his musical forms Mozart preferred to have the basses simple and transparent. He had always loved the dark rich tonal colour of the viola and ... was fascinated by the incalculable difference made to the middle voices by the dazzlingly beautiful web of sound woven by two violas.
>   Jürgen Dohm

1

The darkness that glistens in
a tender look
is lust

      glance which
lighting the air
gives lightness

          so,
in the act of love
we are both hidden
and transparent

the surface of
a deep pool
sunlight ripples,

        hints of
dark gold beneath.

What is the incalculable difference between us
who move to the same end   singularly
and know that we are complex

as the dazzlingly beautiful web of sound
woven by two violas?

2

Stars roar,

                their constellations

incandescent

                flickering hieroglyphs

in which we read no

                sense of urgency

that's not our own.

                They share a

chemistry with us

                who move to the same end

singularly

                but are remote.

Though watched with eyes

                liquid in wonder

they cannot be touched

                    as I touch you.

3

As a stone falls
through light and shade

turning to dark
gold beneath

the surface of
a deep pool

you fall through me
as I think of you.

Coda

If there is a climax
it is one
in an endless line
or history

not ours
and not without end,
who will disperse
in other forms.

The words we have
won't hold for us,
naming an end
that isn't final.

Notions like
'for ever'
are a form of
cowardice. No

image holds.
No matter.
We are here
in nakedness.

Nachtmusik

Night plucks a cello
out of the wood,
deep brown
laid against black.

Mind wants
the thought of you
as tongue wants
your tongue.

Bird-cries,
faint
water-sounds
over the hill.

Night is a deep
slick black
dissolving a pearl
through indigo.

Cwm Cadian

The wind smashes a glass jar against the rocks.

*

Though you are not the subject of my poem, you are in it.

*

To make a physical impression of the lake upon your mind.

Smoky ripples expand like a flower: lines of force. What is it in the relationship of wind to trees, water to wind that tugs at the heart so strongly?

That the spruce is a live creature, responding to air, I saw as we lay beneath it, the whole forest moving, at once in unison and singular.

The fens and the newly-planted tomato fronds tremble. The hillside trembles. As you and I, in desire for each other.

As the words in a sentence conspire together.

*

Time slows. We slow it down.

*

'All the choir of heaven and furniture of earth.'
(Bishop Berkeley)

19.5.73

Polish Rider

The air is cold
outside the Frick
in New York City.

Inside, my heart fills
calm as the look
on the face of Rembrandt's
Polish Rider
who takes his fill
of looking.

Heart, so full
surely you'll break
free at last
of me and everyone

float way
over Central Park
where the eagles crouch,
their bronze wings
brushed with snow?

If only we could see
through this tangled
red complexity
what he is seeing.

Inside his heart
there is a crystal.

Broadway & West 70th

Elgar's mounting cry
breaks my heart
with joy almost
bitter to me.

Hold back just once
those useless
12th floor window tears.
I want to see
clean through this veil
left hanging here.

Shades of Lorca,
Juan Jiménez
teach me your
elegance in despair.

1945

'Writing is a fire.'
                      Blaise
Cendrars wrote that
in 1945.
I don't suppose
I was even crawling then
when he put the match
to his poem
                      in 1945.

He was French.
                      For me
writing is a waterfall
sometimes dry, sometimes wet.

Ode

Trees have their doubts   but we have ours
less earthly. We aim for the stars, thinking

what could be more important to an oak
than the gossip of its neighbours?   To us

such talk is like an acorn, lost in space
to which we distribute our replies

with the nonchalance derived from knowledge:
we are the masters of gravity

not they!   rooted in superstition and
the earth. Strange instructions appear in speech.

'Pass this rubber ball to the willow.'
'The elm has need of a luggage guard.'

These mornings, when the sun rises early
it is difficulty to wake up and go

out to the shed, where you must continue
creating the antiques of the future.

Muted whispering from the stand of pine:
'Here he comes.'   Man, it is true, knows no way

to breathe life into a box   or plant
the legs of chairs. 'He comes' they mutter, and

the wind of disdain in their boughs
has travelled here in answer from the sun.

For Barnett Newman

A profound sense of, well, being
wells up from the sea this morning
to my window in the quiet square
the air cracks and reflects.

Only occasional cries for help
rise from the huge expanse of colour
steady as a canvas by Barnett Newman
taller and wider than a man's reach.

'Why should anybody be afraid
of red, yellow and blue?'
Unzip the alphabets! Unzip the world!
Let eyes and the window overflow.

Two Sonnets

1

Mixed with age, she could foresee the future
Halt between the beds crying, 'Come
Mix with a sailor.' The most beautiful women
Pressed her forehead, little pieces of blue
In the red drawer, holding the wound, burst and
Bloody. It was hazy, up in the tree
She climbed to get a whiff of the islands
Finding them stripped by the storm which is called
The Green Bracelet. She used the Malayan
Word, depicted in dances and the stars
Asking, 'How do I sleep?' Like a round blue
Naked, full of nuts. The past collapsed
With an earthquake close to the town, the past
Smiling absent-mindedly on Java.

2

The professor stood still, tall, thin, with stains
Under the arms, blunt Western nose, resting
On red and gold pillars, drooping moustache
Hiding a few shabby rooms in the shade.
'I am a Christian from out of your past.'
Matthew wore a face in reply. Only
Pauline remained, rumpled, bare feet knotted
With grass, shining orange from a distance
Unchanged beneath the stars. O double-bed
Under the half-dark, where the surf comes in
And women with their passions rule the world
You alone could stop the professor's heart—
Perhaps the sunlight, dark seen from so close
Leaning against a self-rolled cigarette.

Dark &

My dark and cloudy words, they do but hold
The truth, as Cabinets inclose the gold.
     John Bunyan

1

days of rain, last of the year

our children play games in which
well-known securities are rehearsed:
'I am the small puppy
belonging to the mother dog'

a dullness
not reached by music, dope or sex
approximates despair

my poems have been too full
of your absence for years

2

storm in the tree-tops
the sea's great bass

those correspondences
one tires of

won't let you be

great rushing wind
batters the mind
wind, not winde
on the castle-top

take
      oh take them
in the wind's wide mouth

dull words
of used-up passion

spat out
        scattered
on the marshy ground
north of Lewes

3

today I wish
not to describe a feeling
nor circumscribe a mood
(intangibly connected with a loss of self)
but simply to report
from where I stood

'in blank amazement
before the unknown territory of you
enveloped in an endlessly spreading
milky mist'

          years ago
in the distance of a room
your dark eyes, dark hair
wet from washing, pushed back
and falling from behind the ears

only today I understood
in the words of Kobo Abe
how your beauty
pierced my ignorance

outside, the darkness gathered
against the banked-up snow

4

(after John Dowland)

'Welcome
black night'
I welcome you

not because you
purge in sleep
the images of day

but as you contain
what lies
deepest in me

you are its
key
and mirror too

so I was that boy, twelve years old
slipping from his parents' house
who ran naked through the rain
to stand beneath the broken
school-house roof
                    where a spout
gushed cold on his stomach,
quivering sex
             and rolled
in the school-yard pools like a dog
releasing its own secret delight
in black night
             and pouring rain

5

not black, but colour
is a key

not key
        but *door*
not door
        but *gulf*

Joan Miro's
          blue abyss
'free of all associations with the earth'

out of which
through a yellow curtain
a hawk grabbed me
on the edge of sleep
and carried me
to where I could gaze
into the heart of day itself

my own heart
caught in the waves
of longing and fear
not daring to acknowledge
what I had seen
                        night
that stands behind day

lacking in courage
to give myself up

'small blue patch
                in a limitless void'

6

'wing
bird-wing
arch in the smoke'

one feather
I picked up
perfect
grey curve

yellow flash
blown at my
feet
below the sea-wall

I was not thinking
of where I was
grey curve
of ocean
an eyelid's flash

'wing
bird-wing
arch in the smoke'

(homage to Johannes Bobrowski)

The Manual for the Perfect Organisation of Tourneys

for Peter Bailey

1

the mountain

                translucent

in winter sun

shoulder of crystal

it is not, as Henry Miller says
of Capricornians
                that we are
'perpetually bidding goodbye
to all that is terrestrial'
rather
        that everything
– of earth, of sky—
needs us to name it

not that by naming
the nebula in Andromeda
we make it ours
but that
        we can create
(courtesy of George Crumb)
Music of the Starry Night
by covering the piano strings
with sheets of paper

'thereby producing a distortion
when the keys are struck'

the mountain is not
El Capitan
           as Ansel
Adams exactly captures it
nor that loved shape even
changing always, yet
never less than solid
raked by fingers of
evening sun
filtered by shadow
we've watched
                breathless
from the doorway of Taldir

I wrote of it once:
'there is the mountain'
as if to say
           what are you going
to do about it?

irreducible thing
now embedded in
                my self
                your self
the mountain is
inside us

        but not ours

not even that we want
a world to feel at home in
or a world whose natural forms
provide us with an alibi
or a cure for depression

after all
        I ran screaming
off the mountain once
pursued by no phantom
of my own creation
                      rather
a co-creation: mine
and the mountain's

(it was a silent scream)

don't think I'm
turning Platonic

the mountain is there
                right now
with sharp stones,
grass gullies—

        one in particular where
        (I curse myself still)
        I could have made it
        with a girl
                but didn't

        and one where I did
        with someone else
                    in the warm sun—

but can a memory
be that real?

'is it not rather
that art
       rescues nature
from the weary and
sated regards
of our senses?'

(George MacDonald: *Phantastes*)

weary, yes—
              sated, no

2

in the watercolour book you made
your mountain is brown
barely a shape
          a wash
of colour
       and a moon
is rising from behind it

which could be a pearl
or maybe a pear

    depending who
                is looking at it

to me
      it's a tear
derived from sorrow
I planted there
'in fields of light'
on the other side

*

is it 'easier to enter
the most unreal world of the poet
than that of the painter'?

is it 'strange that we can move with such ease
in the atmosphere of words
and with such difficulty among
the almost tangible images of painting'?

René Gimpel thinks so
and sometimes I agree
except that
the world being 'strange'
does not make it unreal
nor is something 'tangible'
therefore to be grasped

3

these days are blank
and are a symptom
like sleeping late
not wanting to rise
despite one's resolution,
itself a symptom
of troubled depression
only temporarily resolved
by dope after breakfast
and then the movies

it seems there may be situations
not covered by the manual

>   Sir Heart sets out
>   all innocent
>   with Ardent Desire
>   but even he
>   (especially he)
>   must drink from the spring
>   the wrong water:
>   thus, the story . . .

but we are too old for that
and wish to speak
only of what is real
despite our dreams
in which we rehearse
old themes of loss
and of betrayal

we stand on the mountain

sunlight

        loosens its grip on

as a jet roars through

our reflections in the lake

from 6 WATERCOLOURS BY PETER BAILEY

1

we read shapes in the clouds which aren't really there?
our lives have shapes which aren't exactly clear
I'm not just speaking for myself (ha ha, you say)
but for all of us here: this cloud must be the shape
of the scar on the leg of a 7 year old girl
whose parents made her stand before a fire
(electric)
because she would not cry when she was whipped

I heard this on the radio today
and wept, and later in the street wept again
32 years old balding in sunglasses
what must people think? 'there goes another drunk'
though I swear I haven't touched a drop all day
and what do my tears do for that small victim
out of the enormous company of victims?
I ask out of my own cloud as I wipe them away

Of Gardens

for Rhiannon

1

lucy curls like a foetus in a deckchair

two sparrows barrack from the apple tree

everything or nothing in the field of vision
could alter in some way this attentive act

soprano and bass pour out entangled sound
as the story of Jenufa enters from the right
over the head of a perfect dandelion ghost
by the bluebell spires

                              whose stems push up
through the pale globe of a starling's skull

2

I want to do away with this 'I'
always demanding to attach itself
to everything that is heard or seen

heavy heads
                of globe peony
nod crimson
              soon to break
in space the blossom
                      makes for itself

wind rushing past
assumes for a moment
the form of the lilac
it moves
         and is moving through

3

shadows of leaves
jostled by wind
from the faint
churrr
of a sparrow's wing
meet the thrust
of a counter-breeze
shaking the waves
of impassioned sound
Janáček sends
through the open door

'a manner of
listening
with the eyes
extending over
a series of years
cumulative
silent
observation'

(Walter Sickert)

4

And because the Breath of Flowers is far sweeter in the Aire (where it comes and goes, like the warbling of Musick) than in the hand, therfore nothing is more fit for that delight, than to know what be the Flowers and the Plants that doe best perfume the Aire.
    Francis Bacon

pulsations of activity
invisible to sight
even in calm repose

chemical storms
and secret influences
whose beauty is crisis
in a formal design
flood through stamen and root

a single space
where line and colour
constantly eliding
remain distinct

each flower and herb
pronounces its name
into the surrounding air

INFAMOUS DOCTRINE

Honeysuckle's siege at the nerve-ends
thickens thought above this bay
to sleepy foam-blossom whiteout.

Ideas tremble at the heart of things
by uncovering we accomplish
intricate reorderings of ourselves.

Sea-thunder speaks with a voice
counterpointing long heat
of insect afternoon.

A man plunges from a cliff
into space he imagines
bisected by cormorants and gulls.

Infamous doctrine may be derived
even from blameless and exact
observation of the course of things.

EXTEMPORE

for Eric Mottram

I will be reborn
                as a bird
Plotinus says
because I love music
                      too much

maybe I'm
          already one
eye winking
                from a black disc
feathers
           ruffled by the wind
I've launched myself on

one for whom
                Debussy says
'music
in an inexhaustible store
of forms
            or pregnant memories'

*

at the kitchen table, writing this
on the first morning of the year
three spears
           of hyacinth
explode in my sight
slow bursts of blue
timed, I swear it

> by the pulse
> > of Eric Dolphy
> whose
> > *Glad to be unhappy*
> is slowly killing me
> > > with joy

Sweet Lucy

'Where does everybody go
after they die?'
is a clear-eyed question
in the voice of a child
six years old
in high-heeled shoes
and a teenage dress.

Bop on, sweet Lucy.
Never die.

A Coupl'a Quips

for Kirk Douglas

It's awful quiet
in the saloon
as Doc Holliday
imbibes his lunch
and the marshal (Earp)
adjusts his granite jaw.

'Mighty rugged
jaw you got there'
Holliday quips
            in the quiet.

Oh place me a call
person to person
to Billy Clanton
            in Paradise
I want to tell him
he did the right thing.

Only the innocent
deserve to die
in this scenario.

The guilty ones
inherit the girl
and the ranch in California
to eke out their
heroic lives
            in decent
child-rearing quiet.

'Too quiet
for Wyatt'
his face in a glass
Doc Holliday quips.

ODE TO MAGNUS VOLK

for Rhiannon

Did you know the inventor, Magnus Volk
had built a car for the Sultan of Turkey
as well as the visionary train? You did?
But then you always did know
exactly what you're doing, whereas I
rarely do.

      I remember, on a bay
in the Sea of Marmara, when the wind
was 'whipping' the little waves
up into bigger ones, and I
was certain that the boat would sink
you just lay there in the bottom, drinking
cold bloody-marys from a thermos flask
as the wind performed arpeggios on the bay
transforming the atmosphere of doom
gloom, BOOM and, poltroon!
into one of hopeful clarity.

                    O my
turgid heart! Yet easily stirred
by the glances that blow across to me from eyes
that are cool, then warm, then cool by the instant . . .

But Magnus Volk! adroit and agile—
how he escaped the machinations
of the Sultan's ageing foster-mother
refusing to commit to paper
his plan for the total conversion
of Istanbul (Constantinople)

to electric power. She owned the major share
in the Istanbul Gas Company.
But he 'with the Bosphorus handy
and knives and sacks plentiful'
sensing in her an Agrippina
who'd learned from her mistakes
fled the country, and thus survived
death by poison, or the dagger
or even the collapsible boat.

As I have survived, thus far
(and so have you) the seizures and the shocks
of a not-quite-yet-completed life.

Transport

I shove in salted crisps by the handful
Washed down with Export, voluptuary
Of the railroad, made dull by the city,
Eyes meeting those of a woman who chews
With slow abandonment a green apple
Down to the core. Outside the coach, the view's

A giant sculpture by John Chamberlain,
The stacked torn bodies of a thousand cars,
Heaped-up trophies of accidental wars
Dedicated to no gods that matter.
By what alchemy do memories drain
Down to the one, retrieved from the spatter,

That lodges? Perhaps how she lifts her arms
Framing her head, the mouth slightly open
Because she has a summer cold, and then
Can breathe more easily (more sexy, too)
Brings back to me your sleepy smile, that warms
The air between us as I gaze at you

A decade and a half ago. Outside
In a field of mares, a stallion stales
With unconcern, as the memory pales,
Fading like smoke-hazed landscapes as they pass.
Head lifted with a flick, his legs splayed wide,
The hot stream pours and bubbles on the grass.

One Way Mirror

1

Are you handsome? Are you bold?
Does your blood run cold
when you think of dying?
What do you think? No
messages to give?
A small residue
Of good intentions.
Beautiful daughters. Two
scored lines
at the corners of the mouth, two
blue eyes
gone out.

2

Spectral trees
painted by Friedrich
but this is England
and I
coastal man
am passing through it
in a rainstorm
in a train
en route for Wales
more rain
and small mountains
whose folded shapes
reflect my brain
whose cells hold
the climbs I've made there
in mist, snow, sun, rain
towards a summit…

if you stay there all night
to watch for day
by dawn you'll be mad
dead
or a poet.

3

Out of the clamorous alarm
mew of a buzzard
and a crescent moon.

★

Eaves drip
in the sun-thaw. Last night's
footprints melt.

★

Ice-bound
mountain wall
under snow clouds.
A gap opens
the shape of my heart
sliced out
with a blade of ice.

★

On Foxes Path
in the stream-bed

mouthing an icicle
rounded by wind.

*

Chocolate and cognac.
Harpsichord and trumpet.
One loud sneeze
Echoes round the cŵm.

*

Stars in your courses
cold in your orders
you will always taunt us.
By naming, we claim you
vaster than man
yet temporary.

4

I must be drunk, it's
1910, home again
with a bottle of wine.
The woman seated
facing me
is Jeanne Moreau
blonde(?) with haggard
lines at the mouth
two blue eyes
closing now
as the train speeds up

slops wine in my beard
soggy as a bog of peat
on the lonely moor
where the only sound
is the drip   drip   drip
of an icicle that melts
on the end of a leech-gatherer's nose ...

Should I casually lean across
to the ageing punk she's travelling with
whispering 'Take care of her'
asleep now, appalled how
dopey I've become
nervous
        oracular
                self-pitying?

Just before home
closing my eyes
an image of the icy ridge
floats two inches in front of me.

Summer in the City

A fine mist falls on my shades as I emerge
Out of the ground at Hamilton Square.
Prismatic sunlight hazes the river.
The city is exciting itself today
Like a woman, half-dressed before a mirror,
One hand buried deep in the placket
Of her foaming, lacy slip.

*

A man sits, gloomy, counting his money.
Across the room, a tender leaf unfurls
On the swiss-cheese plant which turns with the sun.

Outside, rain falls on the blackened walls
Of the newest burned-out building. The holes
Allow the wind to pass unhindered
Preserving from damage the heart-shaped leaves.

*

Why are there no humans in this frame? Where on
Earth, or under it, have they all gone?
Gone into conceptual art, every one.

An empty-headed day. Aunt Freda
Complains about the Pakis up the road.

Sprayed on the empty steel-foundry's wall:
NF! PAKIS GO HOME! WHITES FIRST! OK

*

Harsh words on parting bruise the heart.
They fester in the mind all day.

The city smells of chemical sleep
Blown from the works beside the river.

Commuters on the evening train
Speculate: will the hooligans
Drop a rock on the roof today?

★

Too much coffee bruises the liver.
Sugar works like a mole on the teeth.
PASSIVE CONSUMPTION = OPIUM
Is the message on the shattered plinth
Of the obelisk in the park. Too late?
As kestrel and rat tighten their grip
On the waste land beside the river.

★

Woken by a screaming in the night
Or breath drawn sharp, close to the ear,
You watch the neon sky for hours
As it bleaches to day. Too soon for coffee,
Too late for sleep.
                      Roses in a vase
Prepare their thunder, the dull mutter
Of half-forgotten rumours and regrets.

★

Confined by adolescents to the kitchen
I lock myself in a book
As the beat of heavy metal shakes the house.
They sprawl in the blacked-out room, hands
Locked in hands, hot faces pressed together,
As I read the history of my time
For the key to my past, their future.

*

'Trapped In the Webs Of Capital' could be
The title of this morning's movie
Which has no shining hero, but me
Attempting to balance my accounts.

As I pay in a cheque, the teller
Shrieks with pain. Embarrassed, she explains:
'I just stamped my finger by mistake.'

*

Summer heat brings out the ants
Pouring from pavement-cracks like crazy
Financiers in a panic.
                        Small boys drop
Water and flame down on their backs
Rehearsing for armageddon. Pilots,
Gunners, bombardiers.
                        Humanity!
An ecological disaster.

*

Let's have a little light relief today
From the dull problems of humanity
(Hunger, money, greed, the polluted planet)
And all their trivial concerns (love, hate, lust,
Remorse and betrayal). Instead, let's watch
Ole Doc Sagan's technicolour version
Of how this cosmic showbiz all began.

*

This is one for all you sun-worshippers
Slumped like melting butter in the park,
Some of you sizzling gently in the heat
As you turn a faint, burnt-omelette brown.
You there, with the well-basted pectorals,
Will surely leave a grease-ring on the grass
When the parkie comes to hose you away.

*

Irregular hexagons of chocolate and cream
Unfolding slate-blue diamonds, barred with orange
Between the wings; the small head furry, black and red,
Without expression.   How can a human being know
The joys and sorrows of a moth? Careless, I set it
On the window-ledge, where the back cat, my co-
Assassin, dealt it a less faint-hearted blow.

*

A slim young blonde suddenly appears
In front of David Jones's portrait

Of Petra Gill with roses in the Tate. She
Can't be more than fifteen years
Old (age of my daughter, next birthday).
Am I becoming a second Roman
Polanski, with a bigger waistline, or what?

*

A cat curled on a window cushion
Spies, half-asleep, on the quiet street
Where a leaf falls: he blinks: I walk past.
Wind churns the trees in the park, stirring
The litter on the lake.
      In Lodge Lane
A man flinches from a window where
Behind bars, three dogs bare their teeth.

*

This woman, shrinking from this kneeling man,
Her right leg folded, elegant, beneath her,
Is: *Lady in her chamber, visited*
By her importunate lover.
      But why
Has the artist placed him in such danger,
A half-man, sinking into the carpet,
Helpless beneath her withering glance?

*

Five o'clock forewarning of the heat
Damped by a sudden shower. By eight
The dust blew freely among the leaves

And stale, crumpled papers of the street.
What fear gripped my heart as I sauntered
Beneath the branch of the sycamore?
One vagrant drop splashed down on my face.

from THE SOFA BOOK

A mirror in a square white frame
Stands in the street, reflecting all
That startles it, haphazardly—
Until at last obscured by mist
That drifts in slowly from the sea.

*

A man leans back against a wall
Thin spring sunlight fails to kindle
Though wavelets crimp and dazzle. Two
Coasters leave the distant harbour.
Their smoke-plumes faintly smudge the blue.

*

Could it be that it's the presence
Of observers that determines
The nature of this universe?
The now-you-see-it, now-you-don't
Co-author of this world, this verse.

*

Poems should be precise when dealing
With *things*, the Chinese poet says
(Middle-aged woman's freckled hand
Laid across balding husband's knee)
And reticent about the feeling.

*

Out of a thick pink storm of smother-
Ing blossom from the cherry-tree,
A fist of small brown birds explodes.
All round the world, we humans wait,
Keen to slaughter one another.

*

Blair Peach died with a broken head,
Thus proving that the state keeps order.
The men who killed him lie a-bed,
Driving their fantasies with clubs
Down pavements teeming with disorder.

*

The white-topped breakers come tumbling in.
The waves of sexual jealousy
Break through the body to the brain
To overwhelm the mind's small craft
And mock its careful buoyancy.

*

Intensity! The finest lines
Network the visionary's eyes
For too much staring at the shine's
Given off waves, sunlight and foam,
Searching all ways for that surprise.

*

All night, the noises of the street.
On Brighton beach, at four a.m.,
Water sucks at the pebbly shore.
Seagulls in agitated flight
Anticipate the day's mayhem.

*

'He's in a mood again' she says.
The rabbit, trapped behind his mesh.
He sits for hours, immobilised,
A tongue-tied poet, impotent, dumb,
Mad eyes upon his upturned dish.

*

Chemical stench blows off the river.
In cold blue sunlight, wind's commotion
Jostles the garbage on the waves.
What's left of wealth once built by slaves?
Fragile machinery of ocean.

*

The city is a crowded lift
But you and I step out of it
Onto a gale-swept mountain-top.
With mist, rain, snow, clouds, birds we drift
And float as if our hearts won't stop.

*

Brightoniana

1

At times, I'd like to be a dog.

There were two that summer, alsatians on the green, whose presence would stop me, every time, to watch.

All summer long, their moving was a pleasure, because— that Western word. Sheer distancing inertia of *because*. Beyond its fence, the two dogs moved and mocked.

The sea was tilted, I could almost touch it, leaning from my bench.

2

I swam that summer, every day, twice if the sun was really hot. Off the pebbly beach, covered with flesh. Beyond the groyne, a speedboat with an outboard skidded and bounced.

The water was not like anything. I swam for a time, came out. Who hates just lying in the sun? I do. So dressed and walked home.

That night the Argus told me: SWIMMER LOSES ARM, torn by a boat's propellor-blade, off the beach where I had swum.

3

Very late, a drunk was shouting in the street. Upstairs in my mind I wandered:

I packed a small suitcase, with night-clothes and a book. Out towards the world I strode. Three adults from the hallway watched me go, and then return.

    Much later still, I thought:

why can't we
reach out to it
and touch?

The Poet Virgil Suspended in a Basket
(after Lucas van Leyden)

Up here I hang, for all the populace to see,
And even babes, with chubby fingers, point at me.
Old ladies nudge their neighbours, whispering my name,
Till every street throughout the town applauds my shame.
The merchants and the jealous tradesmen all concur:
I've acted like a witless fool because of her.
'It serves him right, I say, entrapped by female snare.'
'Trust a poet! Their heads are always full of air.'
It was not air but sudden, all-consuming fire
That filled my bursting head with light (or I'm a liar),
When she first cast her bedroom eyes upon my face,
Although I never could distinguish *graze* from *grace*.
'Be here' she said 'beneath my window, prompt at ten,
And I will raise you up, most fortunate of men.'
It must have been the wine we drank (I sank an ocean),
Or else, she slipped into my cup a witch's potion,
That night when we first met. Result? While brain was dulled,
That other, wilful organ blindly rose and swelled.
Up here I have a vantage-point, from where I've watched,
Since yesterday, the hills with fitful moonlight patched,
And heard all night the dogs from sleeping farm-yards howl
And in the streets the randy tom-cats on the prowl.
No drunken revellers, tipped out from the clubs at three,
Looked up above their spinning heads to notice me,
Or if they did, just softly cried: 'Man in the Moon!'
And staggered home to sleep in tousled beds till noon.
I hung here then, and shivered, trembling for the hour
When every citizen would see me in her power,
For she, soon tired of pouring scorn upon my head,
Said sweetly: 'Now, poor fool, I'll leave you for my bed.'
She closed the shutters, calling for her chamber-maid.

I heard their whispered words and then the moans they made.
To think that I, the writer of those epic verses,
Should find myself the victim of a woman's curses,
And treated as that pompous Trojan treated Dido,
Or worse—kept out of doors, like any mutt or Fido.
'Arms and the man I sing…' in voice august and gravid:
I'll write no more of that, I swear (so help me, Ovid),
But rage and curse like any trollop in the street
Who finds her pimping partner's after other meat.
And if they laugh at me, I'll simply fling it back,
And for each blow I get, return another whack.
O God, suppose some wit suggests: 'Let's raise a plaque'. . . ?

By now, ten hours have chimed, since I was left to dangle.
Above the town, the red-tailed kites and jackdaws wrangle.
The night's last jesting owl has hooted in derision
And sparrow's brawl replaced the nightingale's precision.
The dawn by stealth's turned moonlight into day-bright air
And dried the shining dew upon my beard and hair.
My legs have gone to sleep, can't feel them anymore.
Deprived of rest, my weary red-rimmed eyes are sore.
Beneath me, like the drone of swarming honey-bees,
The voices of the crowd rise up, to jeer and tease.
Aloft, a shutter creaks. The people crane their necks.
Guffaws and shrieks escape the lips of either sex.
I raise my head to meet the last indignity—
The contents of a brimming po, tipped over me—
And see the emperor's daughter and her grinning maid
With naked arms entwined and hair all disarrayed.
I curse her, then I mutter, grumbling in my eyrie,
And watch the sweaty populace, now bored and weary,

Drift off down other streets in search of new distraction,
Leaving me to ponder the nature of attraction.

Noonday's solid silence bears down upon the square.
A solitary mongrel sits and scratches there.
I love, that's all, and hate, as some poor poet wrote.
How long must I endure the blow she cruelly smote?

Lines Addressed to Ifor Davies
on his thirty-sixth birthday

The children of two nations wage
A mimic warfare on the lawn.
When two young languages engage
An entente cordiale is born.

The shuttlecock flies through the air
In peaceful imitative flight,
As jets with roaring voices bear
Their visored pilots into night.

We adults round a table sit
With friendly chat and ribald cackle,
Till one loud ego ruins it,
A Mister Hyde who's lost his Jekyll.

O, why our nature's doubled thus
Has puzzled all our deepest thinkers.
Some say, with Plato, it's because
We live upon the earth in blinkers.

Or if we get depressed and shirty
When evil thoughts and deeds befall,
'Just breathe in deep' says Krishnamurti.
'The world's not really there at all.'

Or when you hug, to spread your love,
In king-size bed or sleeping sack,
'Be sure to wear the rubber glove'
Says Bhagwan from the Cadillac.

When Descartes stated 'Cogito ...'
And followed it with '... ergo sum',

Did he perhaps not care to know
The mind's connected to the bum?

Idealists are all the same.
They'd tidy up the world until
All are identical with them.
A difference seems to make them ill.

So may those children on the lawn,
As language thickens year by year,
Beneath the plane-infested dawn
Remember what they mimicked here

And when they reach the adult state
May they refuse all shining halos,
Not tempted to manipulate
Into enlightenment their fellows.

But you, by virtue of whose birth
Today champagne and joy must flow,
Are of the genial of the earth.
On tennis-courts your face will glow

Whether in triumph or defeat,
For like the sun you'll rise again,
Move to the net on flashing feet,
Most mellow, most relaxed of men.

Chateau de Brécy

Half-Baked Juvenile

for Peter Bailey

> I shall come riding my ayah with his tusks adorned with silver bells and ribbons and escorted by a troop of native howdahs richly clad and mounted upon a herd of wild bungalows; and you must be on hand with a few bottles of ghee, for I shall be thirsty.
> Mark Twain to Rudyard Kipling, 1895

One moment I was dreaming, and the next
The boy who took the photo of himself
(All freckles, ancient hair above his brow,
Left ear stuck out much further than the right)
Quite suddenly remembered me. His look,
Already somewhat guarded and perplexed,
Seemed urgently to ask me: 'Who are you?'
As if the answer could but disappoint.
He held the camera in front of him,
Leaned back against the stucco garage-wall
And aimed its beady eye towards his own.
And there a version of himself appeared,
Caught lurking in the mirror of the future,
Who proffered him with outstretched hands a gift
It was not yet the moment to receive.
Beyond, the narrow lawn lay drenched in light,
Its boundary a ditch, stagnant in summer,
Suburban peace fenced off beside a wood
Where rival gangs from temporary camps
Made war, till mothers called them in for tea.

Peter, it was of you that I was thinking
Just now when I sat down to write, before

My dreaming and my teenage selves conspired
To lure me from the present to the past:
How different our early years, and yet
We travelled to a point where pathways crossed.
While I above the city's muffled roar
Tossed restlessly upon a rumpled bed,
Beneath a creaking punkah you slept fast
And dreamed a universe of dark and light,
As brightly-coloured birds outside your window
(The babbler and the bulbul) whistled and flashed.
Or woken by the huge sub-tropic moon
Whose pitted features peered in through the pane,
Wide-eyed you sucked an opiated thumb
And heard the planet breathing as you lay.

One morning I, a serious child, announced
That I was leaving home, and at the door
Stood solemnly, my tiny suitcase packed
With night-clothes and a book, and shook the hand
Of Mother and of Father and of Gran,
Who solemnly agreed that I should go.
They waved to me, as I marched down the street,
Proud victim of some childish slight, who chose
The pain of exile rather than accept
An adult compromise. At the kerb I stopped,
My resolution crumbling as the rush
Of juggernauts and buses blocked my way.
The world was all behind me as I fled
Back to the door, left open, and my room.

Meanwhile, ensconced upon your father's train,
You from the private observation-car
Watched lightning crackling on the track, as miles

And miles of continent unfurled behind.
Snake-like, out of a blottesque cloud it fell,
Linking the violet heavens and the earth
Sketched in with ochre, Mughal-style. And then,
As if there were a world above the sky
Whose waters at full flood burst all their bounds
To drown this puny one, the storm began.
Devas of rain and lightning! Nymphs of heaven!
Who danced for days upon the drumming roof
Of the train that bore the calenturic child.

Now when you rise each morning from your bed,
Do you still heed your ayah's old advice
And sharply tap your shoes upon the floor,
Since childhood's scorpion-bite still keeps its sting?
Or halfway down the stairs do you recall
Through murmured shreds of dream, the dregs of sleep,
A massacre of servants in the kitchen,
Relieved on pushing wide the door to find
(No grinning heads in blood upon the table)
That you're awake, as sunlight floods the room
And all the daytime's reassuring clutter?

Across my desk, that boy still stares at me
With disbelief, as I sit here and fumble
The gift of words he won't accept. 'Why not?'
I ask, as if expecting a reply.
'Ungrateful youth' I mutter, half-aloud,
And smile, to think of all the later joys
This half-baked juvenile has never known.
But then, in foolish middle-age, who else
But he, with dreaming gaze (somewhat perplexed),
Can greet them and not doubt when they dissolve?

So it was he who climbed with you and stood
Beside the force at Gordale Scar, and watched
With you the rainbow-drops descend and shatter,
Until, a little cold and shivering
Beneath those horrid cliffs, we felt the years
And pulled our coats about us to depart.

The Empty Hill

an elegy for Idris Davies, hill-farmer of Waen, Islawrdref

1

Mourn, you buzzards. You ravens, hang your head.
The genius loci of the hills is dead.
You'll hear his tractor rattle past no more
Nor watch him from your zenith, as you pour
Intensity of seeing on the hill,
Transfixing in the searchlight of your will
Stag-beetle, shrew, wild honey-bee and mouse.
You oaks, that hang from crags above his house,
Join with the wind that's moaning through your tops
To sound out your lament, till every copse
Of hazel, rowan, silver-birch and ash
Shakes leaves and tassels as the branches thrash.
And you, Gwynant, whose voice fills night and day
With murmured grieving-notes, as if you'd pray,
Do not subdue your nature but, with loud
Outpouring rush, let fall a rainbow shroud
To clothe the mossy rocks in jewelled light,
For your, and their, and his renewed delight.

2

But is he dead
Who'd leave the hearth
At black of night
For the winding path?

O, if he's dead,
Who'll walk up late

To drop the latch
On the mountain-gate?

But is he dead
Who'd watch all night
The new lambs born
In their red-and-white?

O, if he's dead,
Who'll drive the sheep
To Mawddach vale
From the windy steep?

But is he dead
Who'd eye the crags
For whisps of storm
And the black cloud-swags?

O, if he's dead,
Who now will go
To the mountain-top
Through the pall of snow?

But if he's dead
And in the ground,
What voice is that
Beyond the sound
Of bird on crag,
Water on stone?
Only the wind
In mournful flute
Through hollowed bone
And twisted root

Beneath the sky,
Only the wind
With grieving cry:
O, is he dead?

3

When Catrin rode the tractor to the top,
Ensconced behind your broad brown-coated back,
She watched the sunlight falling on the track
And said: the spinning world won't ever stop.
And as the sound of engine faded out,
We adults in the formal garden knew
The world that she was entering with you
Contained the merest echo of our shout.

Up there, the sun-struck mountain-giants dozed,
Oblivious to the stranger from the town.
All round, the waspish silence waved and buzzed
In day-long heat, stoked up from early dawn.
The years have passed. You've left the mountain-top.
The child's a woman. The world spins without stop.

4

Your photograph has lain upon my desk
Gathering a coat of dust for weeks,
As I have tried to gather, warily,
My memories of you. It is as if
The landscape has a hole in it, a space
(Not emptiness, exactly) that was you.

The print is old and creased, its edges curling,
The colours dulled: a washed-out stony field,
A faded wood. But you still hold a spray
Of hazel, plucked just now (the summer flies!),
And gaze at me, a steady cautious smile.
A second shows you, distant, dogs at heel,
Frozen in mid-stride along the track
Towards the old tin shack the children used
For spying, repository of darkness and
Of bundled hay. The trees are bare. Beyond,
The mountain-curtain seals the valley in.
Above, an ice-blue sky of early spring.
I hear the buzzards calling, way up there.
The iron fence leans drunkenly askew
And casts a shadow like a spider's web
Across the field. What time will you return?

One night, the lamp unlit, we sat and watched
As first the valley, then the far-off wood,
Near field, and lawn, and sky at last dissolved,
And through the mothy night-fall heard the sound
Of iron clashed, as though two armies joined
To fight again their battle in the grove.
Ghost-struck, we stood, and peered into the dark
Until your tractor, rattling chains, drove past.
You waved to us, as you made late for home.
I see you there, at ease within the snug
Back-kitchen-parlour, tucked beneath the hill,
A fire in the range all through the year.
An orphaned lamb (O Blake! we townees thought)
Nuzzles a feeding-bottle. Round your feet,
A sheepdog pup is worrying a shoe.
The television, murmurous with news,

Lights up as distant cities burn. You watch
And shake your head, unable to conceive
The dedication requisite for slaughter,
Though you have witnessed faithfully for years
Both predator and victim on these hills.
Behind the door, your working-coat (the badge
Of winter and of summer) hangs. It trembles,
As wind sifts through and sighs. In memory,
Behind the door, in darkness, let it hang.

All things change and are destroyed. The gales
Of winter overturned Waen Fechan's pines.
Their dying roots still grapple rocks and earth.
The mole now rules the field that you once scythed.
The chapel's been pulled down, where I was wed.
The gate of Taldir's down, a pile of sticks,
And roof-slates lie about the lawn. You're gone.
There's no denying it. Like all the dead,
You left this emptiness of pain behind.
All things must change and be destroyed. The snow
That lingers in the gullies soon will melt.
The river pours unceasingly to feed
The sea you said no man could ever trust.
These hills themselves still shift, slow inch by inch.
One pear tree in the ruined orchard blooms.
The constellations wheel across the sky.
What ease, what consolation, from all this?

Above the trees, a flock of birds dissolves,
Like syllables escaping from a poem
The poet found at last he could not write…

5

When Idris from his lofty seat
Surveys the land spread out below,
From Cadair's crag and riven cliff
To Mawddach where the herons stalk,
The lakes that glitter at his feet
And valleys stretching into haze,
Where woods of oak and sombre larch
Are splashed with rowan's bloody red,
Or under chain-and-padlock ice
The streamlets frozen in mid-rush
Down foothills piled against his flank,
What cloudy visions fill his head?

Does he, with Gwydion and Gwyn,
Still plot the courses of the stars,
Century piled on century,
As constellations overhead
Outwear the braided lives of men?
Can he foretell what is to come,
Whose ancient eyes have seen so much,
Or does this fag-end of an age
Contain such horrors in its store
That he's made dumb by sight of them,
Reduced, like men, to stare wild-eyed
And silently to mimic rage?

Asleep and dreaming in his chair,
His long white beard below his waist,
Does he recall how, long ago,
He stepped from mountain-top to sea,
The sunlight golden in his hair,

And tossed a pebble from his boot
Carelessly away? Now it rests
Above a cliff its balanced tons
A bird alighting might disturb
And down into the valley tumble.
The clouds that gather round his head
Conceal a light more bright than suns.

6

To Mrs May Davies

Those hills that are the small beginnings of a spine
That stretches interlocking spurs from here to Waen
Are visible today, where air and sunlight quiver,
Premonitory minor bumps beyond a street
That peters out in tired ground beside the river.
On such a scrubbed and wind-stripped day as this, they greet
The prisoner in the grimy city with a promise,
Long overdue, now to be kept—if weather holds
And morning does not sour by noon. Behind those folds

Lie hidden cŵms and isolated upland valleys,
Where close-faced men, with ghost-like dogs at heel, make tallies
Of sheep that cling impossibly to cliffs, and watch
With non-committal eyes the shining cars that climb
The road across the pass, or walkers who unlatch
The mountain-gate, to try last season's record time
From peak to peak. At evening, they return to kitchens
Where fuzzy TV screens rehearse the foreign news,
Relayed by satellites, so far above the mews

Of buzzards in the quartered sky, they might be stars,
The newest harbingers of catastrophic wars
To come. And yet, those distant hills were never havens
Where peaceful folk escaped a violent history,
But in the quiet after slaughter, crows and ravens
Picked out the eyes of fallen men, indifferently—
Cymro and Sais, Briton and Roman, all alike.
Now, where they brought the head of Brân, the son of Llyr,
Across the magic land, from cars the tourists peer

And squabbling kids complain: "I'm bored. How far's the sea?
We'll never get to Butlin's Camp in time for tea."
As each succeeding migrant wave collapsed in foam,
It left a jumbled flotsam stranded on the hills
And in the wreckage each invader made a home,
Absorbed by those on whom they thought to try their wills,
A mountain-folk, with rock-like stubbornness to match,
Who shaped the land as it shaped them, boulder and drift.
Largesse of princes terminates in farmer's thrift.

Did you—the grimy streets, the crowds left far behind—
At first resist those voices, carried on the wind,
That taunt the city-bred from every rock and tree?
When snow around the hill-farm swirled, filling the steps
Your husband's morning boot-tracks left, what did you see
Between you and the shadow-wood? Was there perhaps
One moment when, quite suddenly, the place was home?
Or did you stand, remembering beyond a street
The distant hills, snow-flakes blowing about your feet?

7

Wind makes lament.
Heart will not mend.
The empty hill.

Author's Note: Part 5 refers to the giant Idris, who in legend sits on Cadair Idris (the Chair of Idris), the mountain overlooking Waen. Iolo Morganwg in his *Triads of Britain* names him one of 'the three renowned astronomers of the Isle of Britain', along with Gwydion son of Dôn and Gwyn son of Nudd. 'Such was their knowledge of the stars . . . that they could prognosticate whatever was wished to be known unto the day of doom.'

TALKING WITH DEWI

i.m. Dewi-Prys Thomas, architect, 1916–1985

I wonder, did you read the book
By Adrian Stokes, called *Smooth and Rough*,
A title that could well describe
The course of our relationship,
Begun when I, intruding on
Your far seigneurial domain,
First came to Taldir and displayed
A charmless adolescent lust?
Your midnight footsteps in the hall
Should surely have forewarned me I
Was trespassing where I should not,
In dalliance upon the bed
(Well, sleeping-bag upon the floor)
With the dark step-daughter of the king,
Usurping his manorial rights,
Too much at home, too soon, within
His castle-wall. Or worse: just plain
Oblivious of his majesty.

Your edict—that unwanted guests
Should always do the decent thing—
Came to me through byzantine ways:
I left. Proleptic move! And you,
Distributing a wry largesse,
In your own car, right royally,
Processed me to the nearest train.

★

In later years, by marriage made
Familiar of your house, I took

Delight to pit my night visage
Against your own across the room,
Disturber of your solitude
When all the female company
That fluttered to your whim by day
Had been exhausted into bed.
Antagonist! And yet, I shared
With you the calm of summer night,
The lake-side garlanded with lights
All doubled in the watery glass,
And urban dark, insomniac
With distant cars and muffled quacks.

I see you now, beneath the lamp
That seems to hold within its shade
The smoke that rises from your fag,
A small domestic thunder-cloud,
Before which, shortly, I retreat.

Shirt-sleeved, you read into the dawn.

*

Then Taldir, too, became for me
A second home—the Magic Place,
Encircled with a mountain-ring
That seemed to hold at bay all harm—
Until my follies banished me
To exile that was permanent.

No more of that! The maudlin mode
Is not what I set out upon.

I asked you, did you read a book
By Adrian Stokes, called *Smooth and Rough*?
He quotes the words of Doctor Freud:
'A man who doubts his own love may,
Or must, doubt every lesser thing.'
Is that my guilt? Ah, yes. But then,
Don't all we humans live with doubt,
Not only in these squalid times
But ever since the first man-ape
Found fire would scorch and yet was good?
That love could warm and freeze his heart?
First architect, he raised a roof
For shelter, and because he knew
The earth he loved did not love him,
And from his abri on the cliff
Gazed out upon a wilderness
And swore one day it would be his.

★

Daily, you stared up at the hill
Called Gribin, where the folly stood
So perfect in your dreaming eye
It finally was never built.
The wind still combs the crest of pines
Above the clearing, where I watched
The antic gestures of a band
Of madmen dancing in a ring.

One summer, under your command,
We grubbed up bushes, chopped down trees,
Moved stumps and stones, as you stood by
Against a tumbled wall and puffed

Your smoke-wreathed visionary plan.
Result? Much sweat. Some blisters. And,
For me, a wasp-sting on the arm.

Next year, the rhododendron-tide
Swept back and drowned it all, but left
Your hortus siccus high and dry.

*

Each morning, in a reverent hush,
The household waited silently
Your distant bathroom-cough that warned:
The tyrant of the tea-cup stirs.
Perfectionist! You could be gruff,
Were petulant, then charmed, by turns.
Your fulsome rhetoric, Merlin-like,
Could magically empty rooms.

Close reader of the elegy
I wrote upon your neighbour's death,
You poète manqué (self-styled so),
I wonder what you'd make of this
Attempt at talking with the dead
In verse that, while it teases, weeps.
No doubt, we'd argue over words
You'd sat long hours beneath the lamp
Examining with minute care,
As I have done, constructing them.
The poet, like an architect,
Labours to make his poem stand
As firmly in the flux of time
As quarried slate and Cambrian stone.

Cunedda's son, you did not doubt
But kept your father's memory.
You fought the gauleiters of taste
And held the pulsing sinuous line.
Now you and he both occupy
The deep lacuna of the earth.
May rowan-torches blaze the air
Above Rehoboth and your tomb.

The Mountain Suite

What law of geologic time
Accomplished this green sculpted cŵm?
The same that shaped the mouth of ice
The mountain-stream pours from. The same
That shaped this brain-coil and these eyes?

*

Flip-flops, high-heels and varnished boots
Turn Mr. Poucher's safest routes
Into a long lounge-lizard's nightmare.
A mountain doesn't give two hoots
For tap-dancing townees and their footwear.

*

Morning so cool, so calm, so bright!
Your early seventeenth century light
Falls on the mountain in the lake
With scarce a waking soul abroad
To mourn the end you move toward.

*

'Are you one o' them canoeists?'
Old Welsh drunk demands through the mists
That wreathe the Plâs Coch Inn urinal,
Before he slips to the porcelain floor
As the white-water starts to roar.

*

What words to say before the prospect
East and West from the Roman Steps?
Let eyes alone consume each aspect,
As if to permanently bind
Sky, sea and mountains in the mind.

★

Some men draw back before an edge
While others gaze below, their cool
Concern for sandwiches a hedge
Around a fascinated fear,
And wind persuasive at their ear.

★

To share a strange bed with a man
(Iron pillow, short by a foot)
And stub your toe en route to the can
Is not a fate most married males
Are ready to embrace in Wales.

★

INDIAN POLICE PUT OUT THE EYES
OF PRISONERS WITH A CYCLE-SPOKE
The newspaper reports today.
Through thickening dusk, we look and look
As world slips steadily away.

★

A warning to the Admiral
Who breakfasts in the English style
On eggs and bacon, pond'rously.
Young Mr. Harwood eyes with greed
Your three-piece suit of hairy tweed.

*

Fishermen let down lines to where
Once voices sent up curse and prayer.
God gives. The Water Board destroys.
By chapel door and bedroom stair,
Now fish perform their clammy joys.

*

The gap-toothed walls of Dinas Bran
Lean off their hill, as if they grin
At the centuries. A bee drones,
Faint below wind-batter. Happiness?
Something a bee can only guess?

*

Four brave men go up on the mountain
In rain, wind, snow, sunshine and ice.
Much later, they consume a fountain
Of gin and tonic, wine and beer.
Men, and the mountain, disappear.

Two Pieces Of Water For Sally

Pool

Close-up, you photograph a peat-black pool,
The filigree of ice that edges it,
While I continue swearing at a school

Of motor-cycling morons who see fit
To choke the mountain-path with noise and smoke
As if it were their own back-garden. May a pit

Of icy water swallow them and soak
Their monstrous engines so they fail to start.
Too harsh, you say? A reasonable bloke

Should see the other's point of view? What part
Does noble reason play in them? Enough
To fill a petrol-tank and make it fart!

Through mist their raspberries fade. Down from the bluff,
Disgruntled, we descend, until a sweep
Of moorland, rising to a spiky ruff

Of trees upon a distant ridge, one peep
Of temporary brightness just behind,
Lifts us again. No sound, but for the sheep

Whose voices carry faintly down the wind
That's silence to a pair of city ears.
The shutter clicks. How patiently you find

An image which, though fleet, holds fast the years.

Lake

What did you feel? I felt a little fear
As we emerged, through dour and dripping pines,
A pair of comic spies, robbed of our lines
By the frozen lake, so grey and so severe.

We passed the others, huddling down below—
Six hikers (shrouded pairs); a gang of ten
Loud Germans, newly kitted-out; and then
An ad-man's family-group, with dog in tow—

And climbed up through the wood beside a fall.
'More sodding wet!' I secretively swore,
Watching the shameless torrent gush and pour
Out from its shelf. The rain was a funeral pall.

Nobody there! to spy upon the kiss
You placed (because I moved) upon my ear,
But thus you make a wonder of my fear:
I turned my head to catch the faintest hiss

Of rain which danced and sang upon the ice.

Romantic Relics

When Shelley's heart refused to burn
Lord Byron swam a mile from shore
To question ocean and return
With arms and shoulders scorched quite raw.

Poor Percy's heart from hand to hand
By friends was doomed to circulate
As if it had, like monkey-gland,
The power to rejuvenate.

Lord Byron's blistered skin, preserved
Among her relics by his donna,
Is still around to be observed
By scholars, although he's a goner.

My friends, I hope, when I depart
Will find no use for hide or heart.

the countryside, aflame with rumour

www.ingramcontent.com/pod-product-compliance
Lightning Source LLC
Chambersburg PA
CBHW031155160426
43193CB00008B/373